SEAL! TEAM SIX

MELISSA GISH

NORTH
AMERICA

EUROPE

ASIA

AFRICA

SOUTH
AMERICA

AUSTRALIA

CREATIVE EDUCATION · CREATIVE PAPERBACKS

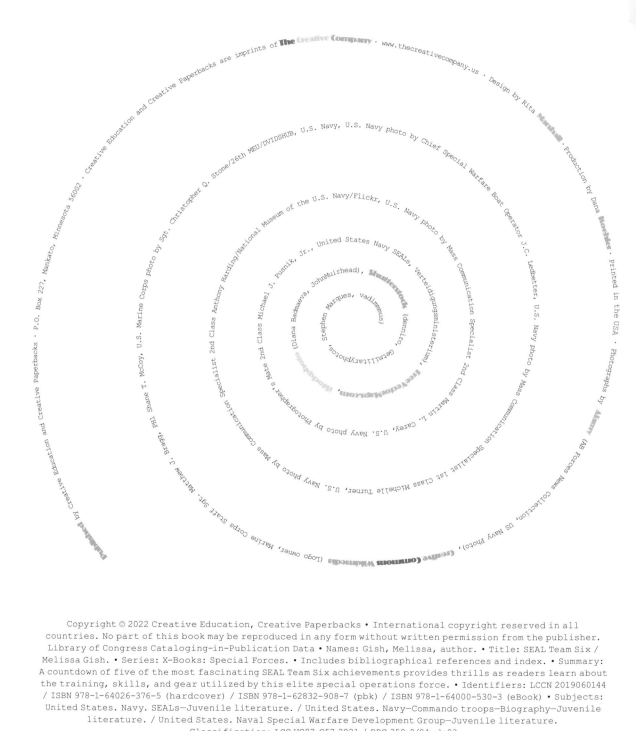

Published by Creative Education and Creative Paperbacks · P.O. Box 227, Mankato, Minnesota 56002 · Creative Education and Creative Paperbacks are imprints of The Creative Company · www.thecreativecompany.us · Design by Rita Marshall · Production by Dana Meuhler · Printed in the USA · Photographs by Alamy (AB Forces News Collection, US Navy photo), Creative Commons Wikimedia (Logo owner, Marine Corps Staff Sgt. Matthew C. Bragg, PH1 Shane T. McCoy, U.S. Marine Corps photo by Sgt. Christopher Q. Stone/26th MEU/DVIDSHUB, U.S. Navy, U.S. Navy photo by Chief Special Warfare Boat Operator J.C. Ledbetter, U.S. Navy photo by Mass Communication Specialist 2nd Class Martin L. Carey, U.S. Navy photo by Mass Communication Specialist 1st Class Michelle Turner, U.S. Navy photo by Photographer's Mate 2nd Class Michael J. Pusnik, Jr., United States Navy SEALs, Verteidigungsministerium), Dreamstime (Diana Badmaeva, JohnMuirhead), Getty (Stephen Marques, vadimmmus), Shutterstock (dennito, GenMilitaryPhotos), freevectormaps.com, Biodidon

Library of Congress Cataloging-in-Publication Data • Names: Gish, Melissa, author. • Title: SEAL Team Six / Melissa Gish. • Series: X-Books: Special Forces. • Includes bibliographical references and index. • Summary: A countdown of five of the most fascinating SEAL Team Six achievements provides thrills as readers learn about the training, skills, and gear utilized by this elite special operations force. • Identifiers: LCCN 2019060144 / ISBN 978-1-64026-376-5 (hardcover) / ISBN 978-1-62832-908-7 (pbk) / ISBN 978-1-64000-530-3 (eBook) • Subjects: United States. Navy. SEALs—Juvenile literature. / United States. Navy—Commando troops—Biography—Juvenile literature. / United States. Naval Special Warfare Development Group—Juvenile literature.
Classification: LCC VG87.G57 2021 / DDC 359.9/84—dc23
CCSS:RI.3.1-8; RI.4.1-5, 7; RI.5.1-3, 8; RI.6.1-2, 4, 7; RH.6-8.3-8

First Edition HC 9 8 7 6 5 4 3 2 1 • First Edition PBK 9 8 7 6 5 4 3 2 1

EAL! TEAM SIX

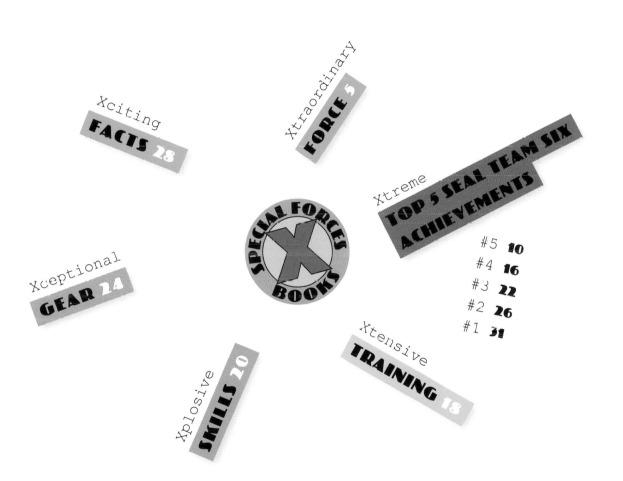

SPECIAL FORCES BOOKS

SEAL TEAM SIX SQUADRONS

ASSAULT

Red Squadron, Blue Squadron

Gold Squadron, Silver Squadron

MOBILITY & TRANSPORTATION

Gray Squadron

RECONNAISSANCE & SURVEILLANCE

Black Squadron

SELECTION & TRAINING

Green Team

XTRAORDINARY FORCE

SEAL Team Six is one of the most highly trained elite forces in the United States military. The team is considered the best of the best.

SEAL Team Six Basics

SEAL Team Six performs demanding operations. Like all U.S. Navy SEAL teams, assignments can take place at sea, in the air, or on land. Missions include eliminating terrorist threats and rescuing hostages.

SEAL Team Six is organized into color-coded squadrons. The four assault squadrons are Red, Blue, Gold, and Silver. To be considered for an assault squadron, candidates must complete a minimum of two combat tours. They also have to serve on a regular SEAL team for at least five years.

SEAL TEAM SIX

SEAL Team Six is headquartered at Dam Neck, Virginia. The team can go anywhere in the world with just a few hours' notice.

VIRGINIA

OPERATION JUST CAUSE

Panama, December 1989– January 1990

OPERATION URGENT FURY

Grenada, October 1983

OPERATION ANACONDA

Afghanistan, March 2002

OPERATION NEPTUNE SPEAR

Pakistan, May 2, 2011

OPERATION CELESTIAL BALANCE

Somalia, September 14, 2009

OPERATION OCTAVE FUSION

Somalia, January 25, 2012

SQUADRON INSIGNIAS

Each squadron has a badge related to its nickname.

Each combat squadron except Silver has a nickname. Red Squadron is known as the "tribe." Gold Squadron is the "knights." Blue Squadron goes by "pirates." Gray Squadron is the "Vikings."

Gray Squadron specializes in transportation. Operators crew high-speed boats. They use parachutes to drop the vessels from cargo planes.

Formerly a sniper unit, Black Squadron focuses on **espionage**. Members of this group engage in advance force operations. This means they conduct **reconnaissance** before attacks. Unlike other squadrons, Black includes female operators. Though not trained as SEALs, Black Squadron operators are highly skilled. They serve as spies and provide support to SEAL Team Six.

Most SEAL Team Six missions remain highly classified.

SECRET X MISSIONS

SEAL TEAM SIX BASICS FACT

About 1,500 support personnel assist roughly 300

SEAL Team Six assault troops.

Xtreme SEAL Team Six Achievement #5

Hell Week Before joining SEAL Team Six, sailors must serve on a regular SEAL team. To join the Navy SEALs, candidates must endure Hell Week. Physically and mentally stressful exercises test their limits. Trainees are allowed little time to sleep. They spend much of the time in the cold waters of the Pacific Ocean. About 70 percent quit. Those who withstand Hell Week are allowed to continue SEAL training.

After passing the 6-month BUD/S course, SEAL recruits undergo more than 18 months of additional training.

SEAL Team Six Beginnings

During World War II (1939-45), specially trained U.S. Navy scouts swam to enemy-held beaches. They searched for information. Eventually, these scouts formed Underwater Demolition Teams (UDTs). UDTs cleared the way for forces coming ashore.

The navy's scouting unit became official in 1962. The first two SEAL teams were established in January that year. The original SEAL team members were former UDTs. They went on hundreds of missions in the Vietnam War (1955-75). By 1980, military officials decided that the navy should form an elite unit that could respond quickly to crisis situations. SEAL Team Six was born.

The team's name served as a trick. Officials hoped to convince America's enemies that five other elite SEAL teams existed. In reality, only the two original SEAL teams were active at that time. The navy renamed the unit in 1987. It became the Naval Special Warfare Development Group, or DEVGRU. Unofficially, the name "SEAL Team Six" has stuck. Some sources suggest that DEVGRU's name was secretly changed yet again.

1962
First two SEAL teams formed

1980
SEAL Team Six formed and trained

1987

SEAL Team Six officially changes name to DEVGRU

2001

SEAL Team Six operations expanded world-wide in response to 9/11 terror attacks

SEAL TEAM SIX BEGINNINGS FACT

Lieutenant commander Richard Marcinko was in charge of developing SEAL Team Six in 1980. He had just six months to get everyone ready.

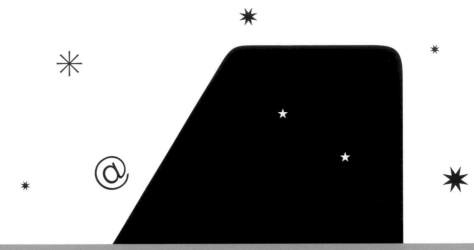

Xtreme SEAL Team Six
Achievement #4

The Best of the Best Green Team oversees
the selection and training of SEAL Team
Six members. Training is exceptionally
challenging. Recruits run and swim daily.
They learn to make split-second choices.
In kill-house training, they move through
buildings filled with "threats" and
"innocents." If a trainee accidentally
shoots a non-threat, Green Team removes
him from the program. Candidates who
fail training return to their previous
positions on other SEAL teams.

XTENSIVE TRAINING

SEAL Team Six candidates must pass a difficult nine-month training program.

They learn to think fast under extreme pressure to save lives.

During training, a hood is placed over a recruit's head. He must instantly respond to whatever scenario he is in when the hood is removed.

SEAL recruits

<1% — 20%

80%

fail training

become SEALs

join SEAL Team Six

Each trainee may fire 1,000 rounds daily.

LOTS OF AMMO

Life as a Trainee

Because of the firm rules for SEAL Team Six consideration, most operators are in their 30s before joining the team. All SEALs are taught close-quarters combat (CQC). They learn how to handle violent conflicts. SERE training teaches SEALs how to avoid being captured and how to survive with few resources. They also learn how to withstand questioning if they are caught.

SEALs must perfect skydiving exercises. They do high altitude, low opening (HALO) and high altitude, high opening (HAHO) jumps. The men jump from more than six miles (9.7 km) above the ground. HALO jumps are especially risky. Parachutes are not opened until about 2,000 feet (610 m). Trainees use special gear to land in exact locations—even under cover of darkness.

XPLOSIVE SKILLS

SEAL Team Six operators are handpicked and highly trained. A combination of experience, continued practice, and teamwork makes the unit exceptionally successful.

SEAL Team Six commonly works with the army's Night Stalkers. This elite helicopter unit flies SEALs to target locations.

XPLOSIVE SKILLS FACT

Gray Squadron is the best at waterborne **insertions** and extractions.

Sliding quickly down a rope is called fast-roping. This allows SEALs to get out of a helicopter that cannot land. SEALs carry all their gear, including military dogs, while fast-roping.

Snipers shoot accurately from far away. They often hide on high ground or rooftops. They wait patiently. The best snipers can hit targets more than 1.2 miles (1.9 km) away.

With practice, SEALs can ignore pain. Operators commonly train and work with battered bodies, broken bones, and concussions. Dealing with pain is part of a SEAL's life.

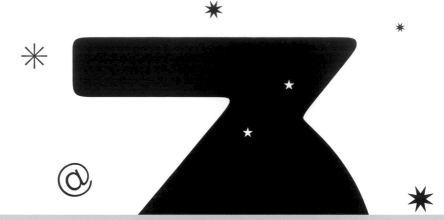

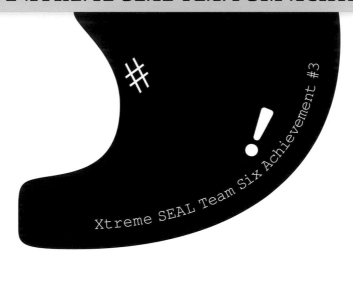

Xtreme SEAL Team Six Achievement #3

Devotion to Duty Edward C. Byers joined the U.S. Navy in 1998. Four years later, he graduated BUD/S. When Dilip Joseph was kidnapped in December 2012, Byers and his team volunteered to rescue the American doctor. The team rushed into a secure building in eastern Afghanistan. Byers fought his way through armed guards and saved the doctor. President Barack Obama awarded Byers the Medal of Honor on February 29, 2016.

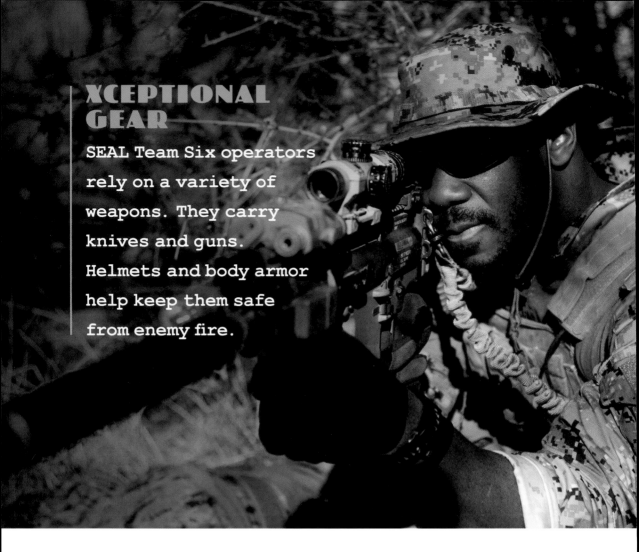

XCEPTIONAL GEAR

SEAL Team Six operators rely on a variety of weapons. They carry knives and guns. Helmets and body armor help keep them safe from enemy fire.

SEAL Team Six Gear

All the unit's weapons have suppressors. These reduce the sound of gunfire and hide the flash from a muzzle. Many firearms can be fitted with a night-vision scope. Bullets fired from submachine guns can travel more than 200 yards (183 m). Snipers often use the McMillan TAC-338. This rifle is four feet (1.2 m) long. It is usually placed on a tripod. Black Squadron spies may carry the SIG Sauer P226. This pistol is less than eight inches (20.3 cm) long.

C6 breaching tape is used to blow open doors. The tape contains a gel-like explosive. It can be quickly stuck on doorframes. This tape can take a door off its hinges.

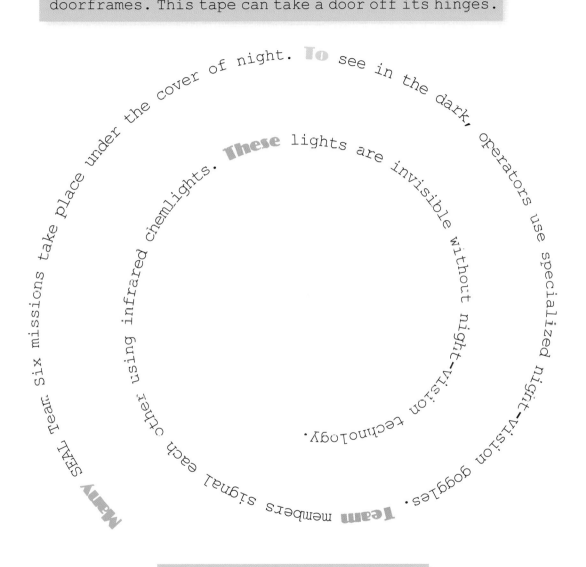

Many SEAL Team Six missions take place under the cover of night. To see in the dark, operators use specialized night-vision goggles. Team members signal each other using infrared chemlights. These lights are invisible without night-vision technology.

Xtreme SEAL Team Six
Achievement #2

Bull Frog Admiral William H. McRaven earned the title of "Bull Frog" in 2011. This name is given to the longest-serving SEAL on active duty. McRaven became a SEAL in 1995. He served in the navy from 1977 until his retirement in 2014. As commander of the U.S. Special Forces, he was one of the chief planners for Operation Neptune Spear. This mission, carried out by SEAL Team Six, resulted in the death of terrorist Osama bin Laden.

Like all Navy SEALS, SEAL Team Six operators are expert swimmers and scuba divers.

SEALs must be able to swim 500 yards (457 m) in less than 8 minutes and run 1.5 miles (2.4 km) in under 9 minutes.

SEAL Team Six is believed to track down dangerous weapons that fall into enemy hands.

Silver Squadron combines imagery from the three other assault squadrons in its logo.

SEALs learn methods of escape as well as how to make weapons from materials at hand.

SEAL Team Six operators are taught to scale, or climb, the walls of buildings.

DEVGRU's motto is "For something greater."

SEALs travel to Alaska to practice survival skills in deep snow and near-freezing water.

Training includes keeping weapons clean and testing gunsights for accuracy.

In 2012, SEAL Team Six operators rescued two kidnapped aid workers in Somalia.

Gold Squadron lost 15 operators when a helicopter was shot down in Afghanistan in 2011.

SEAL Team Six operators fast-roped into Osama bin Laden's compound in Pakistan.

SEAL Team Six was created for "no-fail" missions. Lives often depend on success.

SEAL Team Six is sometimes called on to stop

pirates from stealing merchant ships.

Xtreme SEAL Team Six
Achievement #1

SEAL Dog Cairo, a Belgian Malinois, joined SEAL Team Six on the mission that took down Osama bin Laden. Military dogs are trained to parachute and attack anyone unfamiliar carrying a weapon. They carry cameras that send live images back to the SEALs. This live feed provides critical information. The dogs sniff out threats. After the success of Operation Neptune Spear, president Barack Obama met with SEAL Team Six—including Cairo—to congratulate them.

GLOSSARY

espionage – the practice of spying or using spies to get political or military information

insertions – placing troops into areas; getting troops out is called an extraction

reconnaissance – a search to gain information, usually conducted in secret

RESOURCES

Besel, Jennifer M. *The Navy SEALs*. North Mankato, Minn.: Capstone Press, 2011.

"DEVGRU / SEAL Team Six." American Special Ops. http://www.americanspecialops.com/devgru/.

Newman, Patricia. *Navy SEALs: Elite Operations*. Minneapolis: Lerner, 2014.

INDEX

SEAL Team Six tests new gear that could later be used by all special forces units.